BigYes
LittleYes
HealthyMaybe
StudyGuide

MARK GREENWOOD

Copyright © 2020 Mark Greenwood
revmarkgreenwood.com
Twitter @revgreenie

Published for Mark Greenwood by Verité CM Limited
Worthing, BN12 4BG, UK
veritecm.com
+44 (0)1903 241975

First printed in 2020

The right of Mark Greenwood to be identified as author of this work has been asserted by him in accordance with the Copyright, Designs and Patents Act 1988.

ISBN No. 978-1-910719-92-3

British Library Cataloguing in Publication Data
A catalogue record for this book is available from the British Library.

All rights reserved. No part of this publication may be reproduced or transmitted in any form or by any means, electronic or mechanical including photocopying, recording, or any information storage and retrieval system, without prior permission in writing from the author.

Unless otherwise marked, Scripture quotations are taken from the Holy Bible, New International Version (Anglicised edition), copyright © 1979, 1984, 2011 by Biblica. Used by permission of Hodder & Stoughton Publishers, an Hachette UK company. All rights reserved.

'NIV' is a registered trademark of Biblica UK
trademark number 1448790.

Designed by Ashdown Creative
www.ashdowncreative.co.uk

Printed in England

CONTENTS

Introduction 4

PART

Chapter 1: But it Doesn't Work 7

Chapter 2: Journey – Not Just a Buzz Word 11

Chapter 3: The Big Yes 15

Chapter 4: The Little Yes 19

Chapter 5: The Healthy Maybe 23

PART

Chapter 6: Using BYLYHM in Local Church Evangelism 29

Chapter 7: Using BYLYHM in Community Engagement 33

Chapter 8: Using BYLYHM in Church Planting 37

Chapter 9: Using BYLYHM in Talks 41

Chapter 10: Using BYLYHM in Personal Faith-sharing 45

INTRODUCTION

Welcome to the Big Yes, Little Yes, Healthy Maybe Study Guide. Whether you are using it in a group context or simply on your own, the aim of the guide is to create space to begin to develop the themes raised in the book and, through honest reflection, to enable you to be confident to journey with those who are journeying towards Christ.

The book and study guide aren't meant to place a heavy burden on anyone – quite the opposite. My intention is that they will inspire you to feel you can more effectively help fulfil the Great Commission: to make disciples. I want you to feel you *can* and not that you *must*. I want you to grow in the sheer sense of privilege and not pressure. I want you to do it because you get to and not because you've got to.

Each of the chapters in the guide has a short introduction followed by four questions. I would encourage you to take about 10 minutes per question and try to go beyond your initial thoughts and feelings. After that there is a key verse which informs the prayer that follows it, giving you a means to pray about what we have discussed in a way that is rooted in the scripture.

Each chapter gives a "Going deeper" for you to dig more into evangelism so you can further equip yourself, and then each chapter concludes with a "Going further" practical suggestion to enable you to take some action to move forward. These are just some suggestions but you could also talk to your church leader, friends or people in your group about other ways you might do this.

My prayer for you

"Now may the God of peace, who through the blood of the eternal covenant brought back from the dead our Lord Jesus, that great Shepherd of the sheep, equip you with everything good for doing his will, and may he work in us what is pleasing to him, through Jesus Christ, to whom be glory for ever and ever. Amen." (Hebrews 13:20,21)

PART 1

1
But it Doesn't Work

Have you ever heard the saying, "If it's not broken, don't fix it"? Well if that's true then so is the opposite i.e. if it is broken, fix it. And as was once said, "If your evangelism stops working, don't stop your evangelism, just change your methods." I didn't want my book to be seen as a gimmick or for me to unintentionally suggest that it's as simple as Big Yes, Little Yes, Healthy Maybe! The language has always been about helping us to quantify what happens on a person's journey and how we can interact with that, even helping to activate it and not a "do this and it will solve everything" type of book.

There are many contributing factors (more than I list) as to why we aren't as effective as we could be in our evangelism. In this chapter I discuss areas in which I feel I have something to say. It's so important, therefore, that we start our journey through this book reflecting on these areas.

Here are some questions to help you reflect:

1 How do you feel when the word "evangelism" is mentioned?

___

2 What areas in this chapter do you feel are most true of you?

___

3 What other areas do you think can make evangelism "not work"?

_____
_____
_____
_____
_____
_____
_____

4 What changes do you feel you can begin to make?

_____
_____
_____
_____
_____
_____
_____
_____

> ## Key verse
>
> "Be wise in the way you act towards outsiders; make the most of every opportunity. Let your conversation be always full of grace, seasoned with salt, so that you may know how to answer everyone."
> (Colossians 4:5,6)

Dear God

Thank you that even though you know we won't always get it right you still use us. Help us to be more effective and fruitful in seeing people become disciples. Help us to pay attention to what we may need to change. Help us to have a better understanding of what it means to be fruitful. Help us not to be fearful of sharing our faith. Enable us to be wise in the way we live and talk to others. Amen.

Going deeper

Subscribe and listen to Mark's "The REACH Podcast". This will inspire you as we investigate evangelism in the context of journey.

Going further

Read Chapter 1 again with some friends and see what areas may cause you to think evangelism doesn't work. Come up with some suggestions for dealing with them and then pray together. Then hold each other to account on them.

#WeCan'tCreateSoulsButWeCanCreateJourney

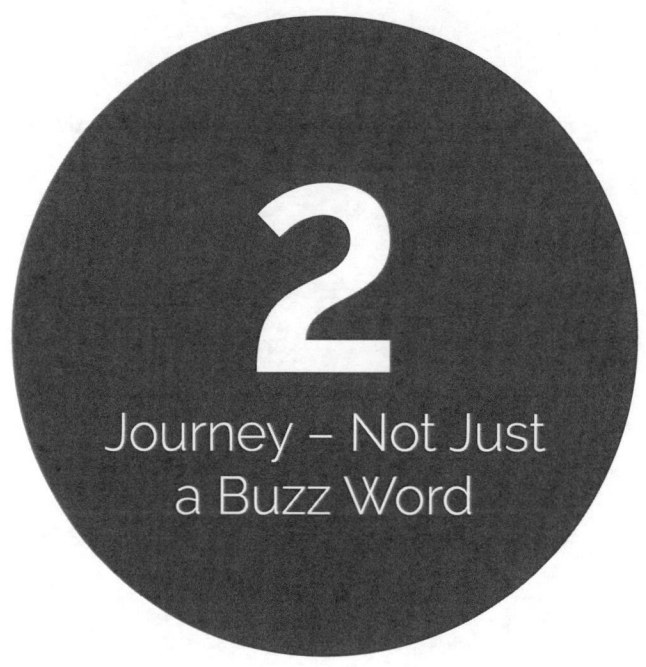

2
Journey – Not Just a Buzz Word

It seems these days as though we are all on a journey! It's definitely become a buzz word. But is it just a word that is in vogue today and won't be tomorrow? Have we simply followed a trend in the church or is there more to it than that? In this chapter we look at the fact that "journey" is more than just a buzz word. It's a biblical principle and one that we need to recover if we are to be truly biblical in how we understand conversion and inform discipleship.

It's worth saying at the moment that a person's journey to faith is invariably a long one. We won't always know what part we join them on that journey and so I think it's really important that we are prepared for the long walk and not the fast sprint. Of course there are exceptions but I would say that in the time that I have been in full-time evangelism I've met relatively few who haven't taken a long time to come to Christ.

Here are some questions to help you reflect:

1 What was your own journey to becoming a Christian?

2 What would you say were the key moments?

3 In what ways are you discouraged as you see those you love not come to Christ?

_____
_____
_____
_____
_____
_____

4 What progression (however small) have you seen in friends and/or family members?

_____
_____
_____
_____
_____
_____
_____

> ## Key verse
>
> *"Paul replied, 'Short time or long – I pray to God that not only you but all who are listening to me today may become what I am, except for these chains.'"*
> (Acts 26:29)

Dear God

We thank you for our own journey to faith and for those who have helped us on it. We thank you for all those who have been patient with us and who have helped us since we became Christians, as well as those you placed alongside us, helping us to become Christians. Lord, help us to be committed to genuine relationships with people who don't know you and, Lord, whether it takes a short amount of time or a long time, we not only pray for them but we commit to them. Amen.

Going deeper

Buy Mark's booklet *Faithbook* which is a guide to sharing your faith with other faiths. It will help you better understand the journey of those in other faiths and it will equip you to share yours well with them. You can buy this at **www.revmarkgreenwood.com**.

Going further

Start to join some more people on their faith journey. Get out and about with people who you know and spend more time with them.

#WeCan'tCreateSoulsButWeCanCreateJourney

3
The Big Yes

Process or crisis? Journey or decision? Should we even do appeals anymore? At the time of writing this study guide I have been a full-time preaching evangelist for coming up to 33 years! Through this time I have heard the validity of preaching the gospel and making appeals questioned in favour of just simply "loving" **people to Christ.**

Now I totally get where the question comes from, and indeed respect the desire behind it, that being not to preach at people at every given moment. The danger, of course, as I often see, is that we can pendulum swing away to correct an imbalance and in doing so create a new imbalance. I want to say that I believe more than ever in the Big Yes moment. We need to create more moments for it, not less, and in this chapter we will take a look at this vital element of our evangelism and a person's journey.

Here are some questions to help you reflect:

1 Who of your friends and family may be close to a Big Yes?

_____
_____
_____
_____
_____
_____
_____

2 When did you last share the gospel with them or pray for an opportunity to do so?

_____
_____
_____
_____
_____
_____
_____

3 How confident do you feel at leading someone into the Big Yes?

_____

_____

_____

_____

_____

_____

4 When you help someone to say a Big Yes, what are the things you feel that they need to know?

_____

_____

_____

_____

_____

_____

> **Key verse**
>
> *"Yet to all who did receive him, to those who believed in his name, he gave the right to become children of God."*
> (John 1:12)

Dear God

God, we thank you that we have said a Big Yes to you and that there are more people across the world than ever saying a Big Yes to you. We pray that you will use us to lead people into a relationship with you. Help us to be bold when we share our faith and to give people an opportunity to say Yes to you. We pray for an increase in our friends and family receiving you, believing in your name and becoming your children. Amen.

Going deeper

Buy Mark's booklet for new Christians called *The Journey*. It is aimed at those who have said a Big Yes but it has also helped many in the Little Yes stage. Buy at least two so that you can journey with someone through it.

Going further

Are there people you have had great conversations with but you've always stopped short of giving them an opportunity to come to Christ? Pray and prepare for conversations with them and ask them if they have ever thought about becoming a Christian.

#WeCan'tCreateSoulsButWeCanCreateJourney

4
The Little Yes

Have you ever been frustrated by how long it takes to see someone come to Christ, especially when you see some really positive movement? You can have a conversation with someone one week and then the next time you chat you begin to wonder what has happened.

The Little Yes phase is often the season where most of the tension in a person's mind can be. We can be guilty of thinking that the spiritual battle is just when someone is saying Yes to God. We can have too short a view on someone "becoming" a Christian. People are becoming Christians in the Little Yes season as they accept and reject numerous times and numerous issues.

In this chapter we want to better understand this season so we can better journey with those who may not be ready to say a Big Yes but they most definitely aren't saying a Big No.

Here are some questions to help you reflect:

1 Who are your Little Yes friends (i.e. they're looking into Christianity)?

2 Who do you think may be ready to become Little Yes?

3 In what ways do you think you have helped or can help your friends journey into Little Yes?

_____
_____
_____
_____
_____
_____
_____

4 How well do you feel you help people investigate/look into Christianity?

_____
_____
_____
_____
_____
_____
_____

> ## Key verse
>
> *"They said to the woman, 'We no longer believe just because of what you said; now we have heard for ourselves, and we know that this man really is the Saviour of the world.'"*
> (John 4:42)

Dear God

Lord, we thank you that it is not dependent upon us to convert people but that it is all between you and them. Lord, we know you use us and we want to be sensitive to your Spirit so we pray that what we say to people will cause them to become Little Yes people, to come and investigate you because we have shared. We pray that those who investigate will believe for themselves that you really are the Saviour of the world but also their Saviour. Help us to help others investigate. Amen.

Going deeper

Buy Mark's book *Now That is a Good Answer* and be better equipped for answering people's questions. This is a key part of the journey in the Little Yes season. You can purchase it at **www.revmarkgreenwood.com**.

Going further

Who are the people in your life that you have had friendly chats with who know that you are a Christian? Why not run Alpha in your home or online and invite them and a few friends onto it?

#WeCan'tCreateSoulsButWeCanCreateJourney

5
The Healthy Maybe

Have you ever heard someone say, "I don't believe in a God like that" and when you chat to them you discover that you also don't believe in a God like that? For many their view of Christianity is built around a media presentation of that view and, sadly, sometimes a Christian who hasn't been the wisest or nicest. Sometimes the Healthy Maybe can be the most significant part of the journey for someone. It may not be a theological decision; it may be philosophical or positional one.

In this chapter we will look at how the Healthy Maybe should not be undervalued. Looking back over the decades I have seen evangelism predominate in the Big Yes and then move to predominating in the Little Yes. I believe we should be doing more evangelism in the Healthy Maybe. I am not saying lessen the Big Yes or the Little Yes but rather bolster the Healthy Maybe.

Here are some questions to help you reflect:

1 Who are the Healthy Maybe people in your life?

2 How does the way you live your life change people's perceptions of Christianity?

3 What can you do to develop more Healthy Maybes?

_____
_____
_____
_____
_____
_____
_____

4 Out of Big Yes, Little Yes and Healthy Maybe, which do you feel you are strongest at?

_____
_____
_____
_____
_____
_____
_____

> ## Key verse
> *"Come, see a man who told me everything I've ever done. Could this be the Messiah?"*
> (John 4:29)

Dear God

Thank you for the incredible moment when you met with this lady and as a result many believed. Thank you that she had the wisdom to simply ask "could this be?" Help us, Lord, to know when we need to be asking more questions as opposed to just telling. Help us, Lord, to know when we need to create the "Is it possible" to encourage and invite many to become open minded about the possibility of you being real, the Saviour of the world. Lord, we know that many of the people we know need to have their perceptions of Christianity changed and so help us to create a community of Heathy Maybes by the way we live.

Going deeper

Download and listen to Mark's apologetics series called "Reason to Believe". You can get these at **www.revmarkgreenwood.com**.

Going further

What about those people you know who don't really know you are a Christian? What about your neighbours? Organise a Christmas soirée and invite them along giving them an invitation to a carol service. You could do the same at Easter with hot cross buns and an Easter invite. Just begin to create some positive connections.

#WeCan'tCreateSoulsButWeCanCreateJourney

PART 2

6
Using BYLYHM in Local Church Evangelism

Someone once said, "The local church is the best boat to fish from." I still believe it. The church is God's primary agent for change and the demonstration of his kingdom in society. Of course, when I say church I mean people but when those who aren't Jesus' followers hear the word "church" they think about buildings.

I've served on a number of church teams and worked with many churches long term and it's my firm belief and experience that people would be willing to come along to church if we invited them to the right thing. In this chapter we consider how we can build a rhythm of events that help people consider faith.

Here are some questions to help you reflect:

1 What type of evangelism – Big Yes, Little Yes, Healthy Maybe – do you think your church is strongest at?

_____
_____
_____
_____
_____
_____

2 What type of evangelism – Big Yes, Little Yes, Healthy Maybe – do you think your church is weakest at?

_____
_____
_____
_____
_____
_____

3 What type of evangelism – Big Yes, Little Yes, Healthy Maybe – do you think you could best help your church to do?

_____
_____
_____
_____
_____
_____
_____

4 What could you do to help strengthen those areas?

_____
_____
_____
_____
_____
_____
_____
_____

Key verse

"Day after day, in the temple courts and from house to house, they never stopped teaching and proclaiming the good news that Jesus is the Messiah."
(Acts 5:42)

Dear God

Lord, we thank you that we are following you today because those early followers were intentional about taking the gospel out into every community and to wherever people were. Lord, help us to have a healthy culture of evangelism in our churches. Help us to take the gospel to people wherever they are. Help us to have varying models that connect and with a commitment that keeps on. Amen.

Going deeper

Visit **www.greatcommission.com** and have a good look at some amazing resources for local church outreach.

Going further

Sign up to get involved in church evangelism. You could even start up some evangelistic ministries like coffee shops, door-to-door, street evangelism. Make sure you chat to the leaders of your church about it and also get some training so that you can do it in the most effective way.

#WeCan'tCreateSoulsButWeCanCreateJourney

7
Using BYLYHM in Community Engagement

Have you ever heard it said, "Preach the gospel and, if necessary, use words"? Often quoted but actually misquoted, this does a disservice to the author as well as the gospel. We must preach the gospel in words and deeds and by the power of the Holy Spirit. All that said, we have had an imbalance in the church for many years where we have either been about words or actions.

In this chapter we will spend some time thinking about community engagement and social action and how it's integral to the gospel. We will consider the impact the church has had in its communities down through the years as well as up-to-date impact.

Here are some questions to help you reflect:

1 What areas of social injustice are you passionate about and in what areas of social justice do you feel you need to educate yourself? Why?

_____
_____
_____
_____
_____
_____

2 What areas of community engagement have you seen be most effective and what criterion have you used to gauge this?

_____
_____
_____
_____
_____
_____

3 What do you feel is the greatest need in your community/town?

_____
_____
_____
_____
_____
_____
_____

4 What do you do to show that you care in your own local community?

_____
_____
_____
_____
_____
_____
_____

> ## Key verse
>
> "You know what has happened throughout the province of Judea, beginning in Galilee after the baptism that John preached – how God anointed Jesus of Nazareth with the Holy Spirit and power, and how he went around doing good and healing all who were under the power of the devil, because God was with him."
> (Acts 10:37,38)

Dear God

Lord, we thank you that you are and have always been kind, that you are moved with compassion when you see those in need. Thank you that all you do is motivated by love for those you have created. Lord, forgive us when we haven't done the same. Help us, Lord, full of the Holy Spirit, to go around doing good just as Jesus did. Help us to demonstrate your kingdom power by being good and full of kindness and generosity. May we be the most caring person our friends and family know. Amen.

Going deeper

There are some amazing organisations that can help establish community engagement projects such as **www.cinnamonnetwork.co.uk** and **roc.uk.com**. Check out their websites and look at their extensive resources.

Going further

Support a community project run by your church or talk to the leaders in your church about setting one up. Or you could join a secular project that is being run in your community and be a Christian presence.

#WeCan'tCreateSoulsButWeCanCreateJourney

8
Using BYLYHM in Church Planting

Have you ever thought about this? The church you attend was once a church plant! If it wasn't for someone going out on a limb then your church wouldn't have been started. There were once no churches in the UK and in fact, had it not been for the day of Pentecost and the church being planted in Jerusalem, Judea, Samaria and the uttermost parts of the earth, we wouldn't have a single church in the UK.

When you mention the words "church planting" I'm sure in most people's minds (and maybe in yours) the default setting is to put another church service in a building in another part of town or another town or city. But is there more to planting churches than simply creating a replica of what we already have? In this chapter we will investigate what it might mean to plant a church and how we might go about doing it.

Here are some questions to help you reflect:

1 How could you and your Christian friends increase "the number of hands you are holding" in your community?

_____
_____
_____
_____
_____
_____

2 What makes a church a church? Numbers? How many? Values? Such as? Activities? Which?

_____
_____
_____
_____
_____
_____
_____

3 If you were to plant a church to reach your friends, what would it look like?

_____
_____
_____
_____
_____
_____
_____

4 What would be the first three or four things you would do to start a new Christian community?

_____
_____
_____
_____
_____
_____
_____

> ## Key verse
>
> *"And I tell you that you are Peter, and on this rock I will build my church, and the gates of Hades will not overcome it."*
> (Matthew 16:18)

Dear God

We thank you that you are building your church both numerically and in maturity. Lord, we don't always see what or where you are building but if your word says that's what you are doing then we chose to believe it. Lord, is there somewhere that we are aware of right now that you want to call a community of Christians to meet to establish what you are building? Do you want me to be a part of it? May we see your church advance in our time. Amen.

Going deeper

Read *How to Pioneer* by David Male. Watch some videos at **www.elim.org.uk/churchplanting** that teach more about church planting.

Going further

Could you begin to think and pray about and around an area where a church plant or fresh expression of church or Christian community could be planted? It could be linked with a community engagement project as we looked at in the previous chapter.

#WeCan'tCreateSoulsButWeCanCreateJourney

9
Using BYLYHM in Talks

But I don't really preach! That may be true but talks are something that we could all do. I feel amazing when I am preaching the gospel, as I proclaim the truth of God's word in front of people who don't know him. There are all sorts of places where we could do a talk and in this chapter we explore different ways of presenting as well as how we can do appeals.

I have coached enough people who were so timid and shy and really didn't think they had it in them to believe that anyone can preach the gospel and, if I am honest, we need more people in our churches who are willing and equipped to do so. Who knows, learn how to preach the gospel and doors may open!

Here are some questions to help you reflect:

1 When you have heard evangelistic talks in your church, what level do you feel they target (Big Yes, Little Yes, Healthy Maybe)?

_____

_____

_____

_____

_____

2 Of the evangelistic talks you have heard, how do you feel they could better help people who aren't ready to commit but aren't saying "No"?

_____

_____

_____

_____

_____

3 How do you think we could change people's perceptions of the Christian faith through our evangelistic talks?

4 How do you think we could better make our talks (evangelistic or non-evangelistic) more relevant to those who we are engaging with (especially since we have more engagement online)?

> ## Key verse
> *"'No one ever spoke the way this man does,' the guards replied."*
> (John 7:46)

Dear God

Thank you that we see in the life of Jesus that his speaking was so relevant both in terms of what he spoke about and how he spoke about it. Thank you that crowds flocked to hear him. Even before he arrived in a town, they were there. We thank you for his use of story and question and that the teachings he uttered are still impacting people today. Lord, enable us, empowered by your Spirit, to be the best communicators of the gospel. May many people respond to it and have their lives turned around. Amen.

Going deeper

Read Andy Stanley's books *Deep and Wide* and *Communicating for a Change*. Both of these are available online at Amazon.

Going further

Talk to your leader about learning to preach the gospel. Start to write a gospel talk. You will need to write it and then preach it in front of someone like your leaders so they can critique it. Try preaching on the streets first or doing a small talk at an outdoor service. Maybe you could organise one.

#WeCan'tCreateSoulsButWeCanCreateJourney

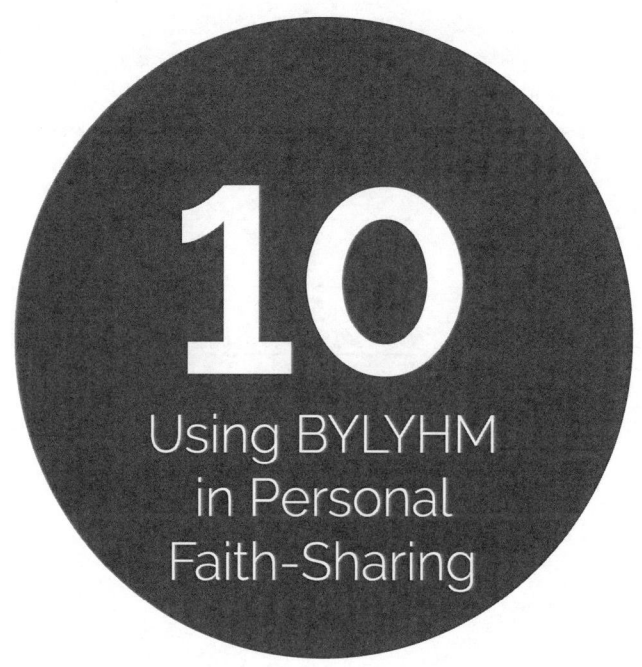

10
Using BYLYHM in Personal Faith-Sharing

Did you know research still shows that by far and away most people come to faith because someone journeys with them? I am more than sure you have heard that statement or supporting statistic to make the case, and of course it's true. I guess faith-sharing is something we have all done and probably think we should do more of, but for all sorts of reasons we don't speak about our faith.

In this chapter we want to take a look at some of the key areas where we can get better at sharing our faith. Areas such as articulating the gospel, telling our story, handling the tricky questions and how we can actually help people to become Christians.

Here are some questions to help you reflect:

1 How does the thought of sharing your faith make you feel?

2 When have you felt happiest in sharing your faith and why do you think this is?

3 Where would you position the faith-sharing you do i.e. are you more of a Healthy Maybe (gently changing people's perceptions), Little Yes (helping people to think it all through) or Big Yes (sharing the whole gospel and giving people opportunity to receive Christ)?

_____
_____
_____
_____
_____

4 How confident are you at sharing in the areas below? Take some time to honestly reflect and think through which area(s) you need to work on (1 = no confidence and 5 = very confident).

i) Sharing the gospel ☐

ii) Sharing your story ☐

iii) Answering tricky questions ☐

iv) Leading someone to Christ ☐

> ## Key verse
>
> *"All this is from God, who reconciled us to himself through Christ and gave us the ministry of reconciliation: that God was reconciling the world to himself in Christ, not counting people's sins against them. And he has committed to us the message of reconciliation."*
> (2 Corinthians 5:18,19)

Dear God

Thank you, God, that you have placed in our hand the ministry and message of reconciliation. That you use us to connect people to you. We know that you have no Plan B and so forgive us when we are overcome by the fear of sharing this message. Lord, I pray that the excitement of the privilege will destroy the fear of the opportunity. May we know that you have chosen to reduce most of your activity on planet earth through us and may we see incredible opportunity and fruit in the years ahead. Amen.

Going deeper

Download and listen to Mark's Boot Camp course on personal faith-sharing. It's available at **www.revmarkgreenwood.com**.

Going further

Get something like *Look Closer* magazine issue 01 from my website www.revmarkgreenwood.com and give it away to someone saying that you would love to know their thoughts on what they read. What about picking up on moments you feel you let pass with friends and family?

#WeCan'tCreateSoulsButWeCanCreateJourney